THE SEA-KING'S DAUGHTER / EUREKA!

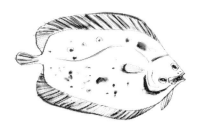

George Mackay Brown

THE SEA-KING'S DAUGHTER

illustration by : ALAN WATSON

EUREKA!

illustration by : ERLEND BROWN

BALNAIN BOOKS

Printed by Billings and Sons Ltd., Worcester
Cover printed by Wood Westworth
Published in 1991
by Balnain Books,
Druim House,
LochLoy Road,
Nairn IV12 5LF

The publisher acknowledges susbsidy from the Scottish
Arts Council towards the publication of this volume.

British Library in Publication Data:
Brown, George Mackay, *1921—*
  Sea-King's daughter & Eureka!
  I. Title
  823.914 [F]

ISBN 1-872557-06-6

Contents: **page:**

THE SEA-KING'S DAUGHTER

EUREKA!

THE
SEA-KING'S
DAUGHTER

DEPARTURE

OLGA said:
Where is he? Where is the good and well-tried skipper, Thord Amundsen? Where is that man, my husband? They drank too many flagons of wine last night, Amundsen and his crew. He's still in his bunk, Thord Amundsen, green in the face. Get up, you toss-pot! The tide turned a half hour ago. Thord Amundsen, the little queen is eager to see the whales and the storm-petrels. Little Margaret, queen, he's a good sailor, you'll have a sweet passage... I'm ashamed to have such a sluggard and a drunkard for a husband.

RAGNA said:

He does well to delay, the skipper. I've seen that sign in the sky a thousand times, the new moon with the eerie rainbow round it. Storms come from that sign in the sky. I'm an old woman — oh, very old! — haven't they brought me here for this one thing, that I can read the signs in the sky and see better than any skipper that's sailed a few trips to Iceland?

Sleep on, Thord the skipper, wait till the new moon shakes off the shadow. The new moon will show a white petal soon... Little one, Margaret, no country ever had such a young pretty queen. It is well for Scotland. There are tears on the cheek of Norway... Yes, my eyes are wet, I don't know why, I haven't wept for sixty years.

I can hear the sailors stirring now.

INGIBIORG said:

The sail's up. Oh what good-looking young sailors! The very best young sailors in Norway. And they look it too. Oh, look at the one with the anchor in his arms! I'm very glad indeed they chose me for the voyage. To be company for the little princess — no, the little queen. I think she doesn't realize it yet, she's queen of Scotland. She's sailing to Scotland to be crowned. It's wasted on a little thing like that. Well, in a way. The sailors with salt in their beards, to her they're nothing special. Oh, that boy at the mast — he melts my heart. Look at that golden head at the helm. Yes, Lady Margaret — I mean your Majesty — we're afloat now. We're drifting out to sea. Are you tired, would you like to go to bed now?

Your cheeks are flushed... That oarsman on the port side, his eye is bluer than any sea.

THE QUEEN said:
Yes, I'm tired. A queen gets tired. She should be in bed. Sunniva should read a story to me, then I'll sleep. How can a girl sleep on a ship? I do not like the sea. The ship's beginning to rock already. Quite gently. If only I could dream the dream I had last night! That was lovely. I was a poor girl living in a forest. I

had a horse and some pigeons. I swept the floor and put logs on the fire. A man came and cut down many trees.

"Why are you felling the trees?" I said.

"To make you a boat," said he, "for you to sail in."

"Where?" said I.

"To the treasure box and the book of laws," said he...

"Don't cut down the trees," I said. "I'm happy here in the forest with my horse, the deer and the pigeons"... Oh, you women, Sunniva and Olga and Sigrid, Ingibiorg, Maria, Ragna — do you know what I'd like to be truly? A poor girl alone in a forest.

SIGRID said:
A poor girl in a forest! Listen to the child. She who's to be the greatest queen in Europe. I have to laugh at her. Yes, your majesty, it's time for you to be in bed. I'll warm some milk, I'll mix some honey in it. That'll make you sleep. The waves will rock you to sleep...

Now then, I must go through the chest once more. To make quite sure. I think nothing has been forgotten. Let me see. The lengths of white linen. The bale of blue silk. The slippers with silver buckles. The pearls for the head-dress. Circle of gold for the wrist, golden clasp for the shoulder...

It would never do, for Scottish ladies to outshine our star of Norway.

Is she asleep? She isn't asleep. A star is glittering in her eye.

SUNNIVA said:
Margaret, little queen, are you asleep? I told you, you'll have a story every evening. Did you think I'd forget the harp? I'll tell you another thing, songs and stories always sound better at sea. Did you know that? Listen:

There was a hunter.
He went hunting in the forest,
The animals ran from his bow.
A fine pheasant sat in a tree.

The hunter's arrow
Quivered deep in the tree trunk.
The young boar
Turned aside from the second arrow.
A stag stood before him.
The sun dazzled through the leaves,
The stag ran free.
Over the fourth arrow
The woodlark trembled.
The woodlark mounted, singing.
His hawk-bound arrow
Struck a bee's nest,
The hunter was splashed with gold.
A wolf
Broke the sixth arrow with the axe of his jaw.
The wood rang with wolf laughter.
The hunter said,
'There'll be worse mockery
When I get back to the hearth
With no meat for the flames.
I'm too gentle a hunter.'
He glimpsed, through the branches,
A young doe in a clearing.

The hunter drew down his face
A black death-mask.
The seventh arrow flew from his bow,
It trembled at the doe's throat.
The doe dropped in the dew and the flowers.
A black shout from the mask!
The masquer stood over the deer.
He flung the black scarf from his face.
There in the forest
Lay a white girl, a branch grown from her side.

There, my dear, you like the sad stories best.
But the sea's different from the forest

MARIA said:
She's asleep now. The queen breathes gently.
Her eyes are closed. The voyage has begun.

Yet think, little queen, that this setting out
is but the shadow of another voyage, another
forth-faring. That true voyage is the voyage
that all must endure, from birth to death.
Great heroes go that voyage, and little children that die soon, and the birds and plants

and animals. All is venturing, a fair unfolding: but the voyaging of the sons and daughters of Eve are beset with dangers, with rock and whirlpool, with black winds and sea-whelmings, with bergs and monsters of the deep. Yet is the chart true, that should bring our souls to the promised haven, where wait on the shore an innumerable bright host to greet us. And one of that heavenly host has been sent out to stand ever at our shoulder, never so true as when sea and sky, black quern stones, whirl our ship...

She's asleep. The queen of Scotland sleeps well. Star-shine is on her face.

Her breath has a different rhythm from the ocean rhythm. Our Lady, Star of the Sea, shine for Margaret.

O C E A N

OLGA said:
Sun on the waters. A torrent of gold.

No wind. The sails flap idly.

There they go again, throwing dice on the deck. Some sailors.

No, Thord Amundsen, I don't want you. Go and throw dice with the men.

Little Margaret, queen, I told you the sea is beautiful. Now you can walk across the cabin without lurching.

Still and all, if there isn't a wind soon, we'll never see Scotland.

Throw dice, Thord Amundsen. I'll eat with the women.

R A G N A   s a i d :
No wind? Don't let that worry you. There'll be wind all right, a gale and a tempest.

Never trust the sea when she gleams and murmurs like this.

She's thinking up something.

The old mother, the sea. How she loves her sons. The treasures she gives them — fish and whales, salt and pearls. Best of all, the stories and the poems.

How is it with you today, little queen? A laugh and a dance. There's a time to laugh and dance.

There's a time to drown.

The old mother won't let them go. She takes them back. She blocks the mouth with salt.

Not yet, old mother. Not this voyage. Not till we set the queen ashore on the steps of Leith.

I was never so shamed. I'll never be able to raise my head on this ship again. The women smirking all round me, then turning away.

I could weep. The girls from the north don't weep.

Make your face a stone.

I went down to the well of the ship. The young golden sailor was splicing a rope. The sun was down. The lantern threw such richness over him....

Oh Maggie, dear friend — I mean, your Majesty — sad? I look sad? No... It's only... it's only that the sailors have such hard cruel lives..... Yes, such a blue and golden sea.

I stammered a few words to the sailor.

Then that shout from the bridge — "Leave the sailors alone! Get back to your cabin, you slut!"

Then all the women at the rail laughing.

All but Maggie. All but the little queen. She was asleep.

THE QUEEN said:
I didn't know this. Not in my wildest dreams.
That the sea is so gentle, magical, beautiful.
Oh, I wish this voyage could go on for ever.
I can sail beween Norway and Scotland three
or four times a year. Who said I'd be sick most
of the time? The salt air has made me hungry.
Oh, I was never so hungry. Never.

They catch herring in the net. Was never a
fish so sweet in the mouth. Thank you,
woodman, for cutting down trees. Thank
you, shipwright, for building this beautiful
house-of the-sea.

Oh, Olga and Sigrid and Ingibiorg, Maria,
Ragna, Sunniva, don't let me fall asleep early.
I want to see the moon on the waters.

SIGRID said:
I hope the Scots ladies, them in the castle,
know what they're about. Will they know
how a queen is to be received? Will they have
proper silks and silver to lay out? Have they
heard how delicate she is, our little Margaret?
I have a list of the herbs and roots. Do the

Edinburgh doctors know what they're about?
This for her cough, this for her cramp in the
stomach, this for her headache. I should be
with her always. Alas!

Well, I won't be ashamed when we open
the queen's chest. The golden combs, the
onyx and jade, sapphire and pearl. Such
lovely droppings and hangings!

I think she'll marry the English prince,
Edward.

No, your majesty, you must go to bed now.
The moon won't be up for an hour. Sleep's
at your eyes like bees. Come now. Unlace.

What does she want to see the moon for?
Any milkmaid can look at the moon....

SUNNIVA said:
Asleep, little Margaret? Waken up. You
haven't heard your story. Don't be angry.
What story? The hunter and the doe and the
girl with the arrow in her heart.

The princess rode through the forest,
The hawk on her wrist.
The princess rode beside the sea.
The sea queen saw her.
The sea queen, witch of the west, was jealous.
'This one will snare my sons,
The sea princes,
They will turn from their mother.'
With a lacing of spindrift
The princess was changed to a deer.
The horse pined at the sea caves.
Her hawk flew to the mountain.
The princess went, a doe, through the forest.
Her heart was a bud of yearning,
A knotted rose.
The great stag turned from her.
She glimpsed through green branches
A young hunter.
The bud yearned for a red breaking
There, beside the twelve oaks.
It came, swift as a thought, the arrow,

The heart opened,

The petals fell in a quick, red torrent.

The hunter sounded his horn.

There, my dear, what could be sadder than that?

She's asleep. I might have saved my breath. There's the moon in the cabin window. She cries out in her sleep. A silver arrow or a moan.

M A R I A   s a i d :

We think of the true voyage — this being but a shadow — only in times of great joy or great sorrow. Then is the chart unrolled before us plain.

On this halcyon sea, we are content with the star gleam on the waters, the sons of a seaman, the cry of nightbirds.

Who waits on a jetty, on a headland? A merchant waits, with a bag of silver, in Lubeck or Grimsby.

Listen. A woman is waiting on the shore of Galilee. A fishing boat is out. She waits. A low growl in the throat of the wind. She shades her eyes seawards.

In Holyrood of Edinburgh they unlock the chest where a crown is kept. A pilot sails from Fife.

She stands, Queen of Heaven, at a shore in a gathering storm.

Our Lady, protect this little queen.

Good angel, stand at her bed.

S T O R M

OLGA said:
I did not know the sea could have such rages.
But I will say nothing. I am the skipper's wife.
I'm a daughter of fishermen.

Thord Amundsen, is your strong fist on the
helm? Thord, I yelled plenty at you, in our
house on the coast. Thord, if I shrieked at you
in this storm, you would hear nothing.

Take the salt out of your eyes, Thord. Steer
well.

Little queen, this is a fine troubling, this is
a merry dance. You do well to smile. You are
a queen of this sea, too.

Thord, I begin to be ill. Come to me now.
No, you fool. Stand where you are. Keep the
helm.

RAGNA said:

Pooh! A storm on the sea. A ship on a rock. Drowning.

What's that?

I would rather drink salt and die that way than mumble for a winter or two beside the fire and be fed from the broth bowl by some daughter-in-law, till the lamp gutters.

I have to laugh, looking at the misery faces...

Such fine ladies yesterday, and the sun on the waters.

The little Margaret, she's excited, I think she likes it.

Well done, you're a daughter of sea-kings, little one. Clap your hands. Laugh.

If the storm worsens, the ship won't live. That she might strike a rock suddenly. A swift salt clean end. Sharp rock — a sea shearing.

INGIBIORG said:

I want nothing. I want to die. I don't even want the boy with the golden beard. Death

is a good friend. Once you get the first kiss
of him.

They staked a wife in the ebb. A witch.
Once. I saw that. Sea covered her.

Oh no! I am young. I didn't want to sail on
this ship.

My mother: "Such an honour to sail with
a queen!" The little brat. The sea shouts. She
dances.

Your majesty, I've felt better in my time. I
thank you.

I've done this, I've done that, such bad
things. I stole a silver coin, once.

A poor man in Scotland will get a sovereign
in his hand.

Nothing matters.

Death, come. Put the cinders and the
penny in my mouth. Soon.

THE QUEEN said:
I didn't know it would be like this.

Nobody told me.

Oh, I was never so happy!

My women — their mouths are gray and stiff.

I went out of the cabin.

They couldn't stop me.

I went out of the cabin, alone.

A wave soaked me, through and through. A big wave.

My coat's heavy with salt.

Out on the deck, alone.

A sailor was sick.

The ship threw me this way and that.

I came to the skipper. Thord Amundsen. A good man.

"Child," he said, "go back to your cabin"...

"Steer the ship well, Thord Amundsen," I said. "The queen commands it."

He laughed. His face was a salt mask.

Oh, I should have sat with the skipper.

They lie, moaning worse than ever, in the royal cabin.

S I G R I D   s a i d :
Safe enough. They're all safe, the gowns and
the jewels. Safely stowed. Double locked.

All else lost, this chest will come to shore.
I lie with my arms across it.
I haven't looked to the queen for an hour.
Leave her.

Others than I will look to the queen. One
in a seamless splendour flowing sits at her
head — so that nun says. The queen sleeps.

The gold trundles in the chest.

Margaret, where have you been? Sodden
and soaking. Not I will answer for this.
Talking to sailors. Get that coat off. Get into
your bunk. I'll rub you dry. I won't answer
for this, I'm too sick. I can't be everywhere.
Be warm, little queen.

Some one will answer for this.

No, the key's on the chain round my neck.
The treasure's safe. I do my duty.

SUNNIVA said:
Story?

I can't tell a story.
My mouth's too stiff and cold.
The stories are locked in me, deep.
Who'd hear a story, in this hurly-burly?
Well, listen:
THE SONG OF THE ARROW—
Thus sang the arrow
Between the hunter's bow and the heart of the
                                                  deer.

'They have broken me, a branch
From my mother, the oak.
They have stripped the green leaves from me.
They have put their whetted knives
About me, this way and that.
They have put sharpness on me.
I was happy in the forest, wearing leaves.
I do not want to be a bird.
Now I am coming to you, little deer,
For refuge and keeping.
Did you not browse on my branches last
                                                  summer?

Take me to your heart.
They will not find me there.
Answer my song with one cold cry.'

The young deer
Leapt gladly to meet the arrow.

After the sound of the horn
A girl walked on the shore,
A girl with a wound,
And a black ship waited for her at the headland.

I have no more stories. Not even for a queen. My mouth is sour with the sea. Silence! Oh, be quiet, child. Say your prayers. Sleep.

MARIA said:
I twist the rosary about my fingers till they're bleeding.

Oh, it is not so easy, the breaking and the

drowning.

The body we live in is a familiar house, with fire and windows, furnishings, all things set in order, the walls and the floors swept, the seven jars on the shelf.

Let but the cornerstone shift.

Let but the roofbeam creak.

We bar the shuddering door.

Where is our quest, the bright one, the guardian, who sits at our table?

He is immortal. The tempest is nothing to him. He will outlast the wreckage. Only let me be safe in my quiet house!

Now, my good angel, whom God has appointed to be my guardian, watch over me.

Watch over the queen.

Watch over the ship. Bless this voyage.

S H A D O W

OLGA said:
Blown off course! I should think we're blown
off-course, with that fool of a man at the helm.
Thord Amundsen. I should think we're
nearer Iceland than Scotland. A good skipper,
he'd have made allowances. For a south-eas-
terly. Wouldn't he? He would. Well, he's
sleeping now, after the storm, Thord. It's time
he got his head down, I suppose. That boy
with the golden beard's at the helm. I hope
he knows his job. Little queen, you're sleeping long this morning. You were like my
Thord while the gale lasted. You never closed
a eye... Is *'Boreas'* headed south, golden-head,
for Scotland.

RAGNA said:

Old mother, old sea, you're smiling again.
Another mask. All gentlness, sweetness, light.

Kindly you cradle the ship. Was never a
better mother to her children. Young mother,
sea that is fresher and brighter than all her
children.

Rock us gently.

The great ice birds are flying south. Follow.

Look at the little queen?

Why should I look at her?

For that I have looked a many a time on
them that behold the new light, wailing, and
them that are soon lo lose the light, and wail
again. We live between two bitter cries.

Your majesty, I am looking at your young
face. Your eyelids tremble. May it be well
with you.

I will know Scotland when I see it, a poor
flat coast.

INGIBIORG said:

Such a draught in the cabin!.. The wind

wrenched the door from its frame.

Look at the candle on the wall. All twisted. 'Never leave the princess... Be with the young queen always'... So they told me, over and over.

Well, she's asleep now, oceans deep.

She looked after herself well enough in the storm, our little queen. She was here, there, everywhere, all over the ship, chasing herself like a kitten's tail. And I sick as a hound, two nights and days.

Sleep, Margaret. Do you have a thorn in your throat? Your breath comes so broken...

I don't need to bide in this twisted cabin.

Oh, he's there, look, at the helm, the golden one. Wave to him, Ingibiorg.

He looks south. Cold-eyed, southward he steers.

THE QUEEN said:
Oh, faster.

Surely the sledge will go faster than this.

Are the horses so tired?

My father said —

What did King Erik say?

'You must get to the inn before night.'

That's what he said.

Whip up the horses.

The sun's behind the mountain. Hurry.

Did we stay too long at the fair?

I think we stayed too long.

I loved the fairground.

I loved the fiddle. I loved the woman with the apples. I loved the old skipper that told stories. Tord. That was his name.

I loved the fair: the fire in its cage, the chestnuts.

I loved the peasants. They danced. An old woman read my hand. She wept.

I loved the laughter and the tears.

Turn the horses!

I am the queen. I order you, coachman, turn the sledge round...

He's muffled. My voice is so small. He hears nothing.

Is there no end to this forest?

I don't want to get to that inn. Bowing and scraping. Gold cups. Silver spoons. False smiles... Good lost folk at the fair, my love is for you.

I knew it. We're late. There's the first star, through the branches.

I think we've lost the way.

'Coachman, are you sure this is the road?'

Let him not turn round. Oh, let him drive straight on! If he turns his head, I'll see, by the light of that star, a skull...

The inn now. One lantern at the gate. Shadows. They wait.

S I G R I D s a i d :
Your majesty, I'm lighting the candle. The sun's down. I've straightened the lamp at the wall. The sea's calm as silk unwound from a bolt.

You've slept a night and a day since the storm ended. Now it's night again. You've eaten nothing.

I'll heat some broth.

She sleeps still.

She talks and talks in her sleep. The fair and the inn. The forest. The star and the skull. Over and over. The lantern. The shadow.

Your majesty, we're bound for no inn, I assure you. We're bound for a royal palace in Scotland. The sea's calm. The wind's fair.

Her breath comes fast and broken

The dream excites her.

She was too long out in that storm. Such sheets of spindrift!

Oh, look at the gush of sweat on her face! Now I've lost the kerchief.

Not that common linen, woman. Go to the chest. Look for a silk napkin.

SUNNIVA said:
A road. A dark coachman. The inn of night. Behind, the fairground of music and dancing. Very far back, the king's blessing.

She needs no story from me.

She tells her own burning story, between bursts of coughing. Over and over. And there, a fleck of blood at the mouth.

Oh, Margaret, little queen...

But this is nothing. A little fever. You'll be well soon.

None so brave as you in that storm.

What's a story but lies — a few bits of broken breath?

No child, a story is... oh, how should I put it?.. a story is a treaty between us and all the creatures. That we belong to one another. That we're parts of a single web, most subtle and delicate. Who strikes the seal on the rock makes a gash in the world. Who puts an axe to a tree wounds stone and star and himself.

Gentle one, the queen and the girl that sings for a penny at the fair are sisters. And the deer is their sister, and the fish, and the hawk in the cloud.

Child, if you have understood this you have understood all. It is time to go.

Blood must flow. The plant must be uprooted. Yet the man must ask forgiveness of the deer and the oak.

There *is* a jar of balm. The story, the music, the image.

Do you understand that, little queen? You will be better in the morning. There are seventy long years for you to understand.

What, the inn in all this darkness?

You are on a ship. I told you so. I broke off my story last night. The wounded girl — she came to a ship... The skipper has said, "Welcome, lady. I am to take you to Scotland, to the throne of your ancestors"

I think we will see the coast of Scotland at dawn.

Oh, Olga, Ragna, come now! Her mouth is full of blood.

M A R I A   s a i d :
A thread of blood. A little rupture in the lung. A heart-petal.

So it begins. So the web of the body unwinds. A thread frets, breaks.

Queen or fish-girl, it makes no difference.

The worm has got in. "In the night, in the

storm." The worm feasts deep.

Does it matter, so the soul has its garment laid out fair and seamless, whiter than dew?

It does not matter.

Hands of maiden and angel have woven the brightness together. They glance at each other, across the white stretch. They smile.

No, it is a piteous cry in the mouth of the girl now. She does not wish to leave her house, the little royal bower.

Queen of angels, comfort her in her agony.

A bird, sea-battered, sits in the window ledge. A shore bird.

It looks at her.

It shrieks. It flies away.

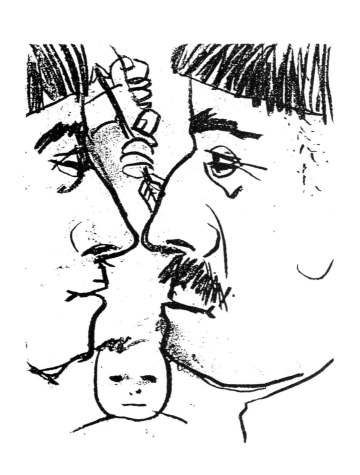

L A N D F A L L

O L G A   s a i d :
There it is, look! A low line in the south. No
thicker than a thread. Scotland.

Thord Amundsen has been looking there
this long while. Eyes thin as knives.

Orkney.

The ship surges on.

Whitemaas falter and fall about the stern.
One rises to take the crust.

Queen Margaret, you should be up and
throwing bread to the gulls.

Will she break bread again?

The bishop has been with her for an hour.
The last oil. Viaticum.

Oh, she'll get over this. She's young. The queen has come to her land. That will give her strength.

The islands have shifted. Another long low thread. Rinansay. Sanday.

She'll begin to talk soon. She'll laugh. That dance of hers!

RAGNA said:
What now, little queen?   I'm holding the mirror to your face, not to admire yourself. There'll be no more of that vanity.

But that a breath might mist the glass.

Nothing.

I tell you this, solemnly. You're well by with it. To grow old isn't worth it. Too much pain, years long, for a few grains of wisdom. If you can call it that.

Beauty, innocence. They burn in the slow fires of time. Ash-gray.

Frozen in wonderment, the eyes.

They haven't closed the eyes.

INGIBIORG *said:*
Now the sailors are coming. They will take
their leave.

It is time to be going.

They come one by one.

Old Amundsen, the skipper — I did not
think to see tears on that face.

He kneels. He kisses the cold hand.

Now the helmsman. His face is a stone.

Now the man that sews the sails.

Now the boy that scrubs the deck. The boy
with the bailing can. He cries.

They don't kiss the queen. They touch her
hand. They turn away.

Now golden-beard, kneeling.

You fool, a live skivvy is better than a dead
queen. His rich mouth kisses the cold hand.

Now the cook.

Now the man with hammer and saw, the
carpenter.

Now the fool of a doctor that let her die.

They touch the hand that's colder than ice.

The bishop has come back. He's lighting a candle at her head. Now he sets a candle at her feet.

Now the harper has come.

He will make the dance for a dead queen.

WHERE THE QUEEN WOULD HAVE SPOKEN, THERE IS SILENCE. THEN THE SILENCE CHANGES TO THE MUSIC OF A REQUIEM.

SIGRID said:
That old queen, and the Swedish princess, and the two old countesses in Denmark, that died last winter.

Well, I had no trouble with them.

Their shrouds had lain folded for fifty years.

There they lay, in their long shrouds, stern

proud ladies.

Inside, hidden, the fester had begun. The slow worm-feast.

But all well in the end.

Earth, air, water, fire: all find their way back to the first four things.

What for this little queen?

Too young.

When a girl is born, the old ones think it time to begin to weave a shroud.

Will she wear her dancing coat?

There's the green dress she wore to ride in the forest.

Always, for summer, she went in yellow.

Here's the bride dress at the bottom of the kist. White as snow. It has buttons like lilies and stars.

Put it on her soon.

The black bridegroom walked through the ship last night.

What ring for her finger?

Look — she's begun to smile! The small dimples are on her face.

SUNNIVA said:
Your ear is locked.

Can I tell a story to a stone ear?

The anchor's down. The sail's furled. The ship rides quiet.

Here, in Ronaldsay, in the earldom of Orkney, in the kingdom of Scotland, I will tell you a story that is not a story.

The girl with the wound lay dead. A girl or a deer or a dove? What does it matter? Waves or branches, what does it matter?

The beautiful creature lay dead.

Grief in the forest, on the ocean, in a hall with fire and lamps.

Leaves fell. Waves broke. A mound of earth was made.

The creature was hidden away.

Then it was winter. Snow, stars, bare branches.

Many winters.

She is forgotten. She is a thin thought in the mind of the last creature.

Nothing.

She returns. In spring, she returns. Cluster
of raindrops, throbbing well-head, the little
burn that runs down to the sea.

She is back. A grass-blade breaks a lingering
crumb of snow. The daffodils light their candles in the March wind. The ploughman is out
with his ox and his furrows.

She burns, a little lamp in a fisherman's
window, she is the fire on the hearth.

Grace of wind on the water. Whisper of
·wind in the new barley, bright air that fills a
small sail in the west, when fish flow into the
net.

Nothing dies.

Yet I must weep, putting a last kiss on your
small cold mouth.

MARIA said:
Go out, little queen. The bright one has you
by the hand. The word has gone before him.

Begin your circlings, hosts of angels, now.

(They don't sound such trumpets on the

shore of Leith. They stand there in Edinburgh, in the mist and the cold rain, grumbling. "How can she govern us, a child queen?" Councillors wait, cunning as foxes. "She will come soon. We will twist her this way and that, like a doll made of straw"... They will be poor and hungry always.)

You do well. Margaret, queen, not to wear out in a place like that.

Where now? Where are you now? I can't follow you into all that brightness.

We know only images and shadows. We go blundering among them for seventy winters.

An arch and a casement and a garden! The good angel has brought you to a door, up from the ship and the anchorage. Sound of a harp inside — great stirrings — voices and footsteps about a long table, jars, fragrance of bread, fragrance of sandalwood, fragrance of water poured for the bruised feet of a voyager. The talk and laughter dwindle. The bearers of bread and wine stand this way and that, on a sudden they make a silence, their hands fold and unfold like flowers.

One will come down soon.

Now the harp again — listen! — and voices of children in the gallery.

Not for us here. Not yet.

"Hail, our life our sweetness and our hope. To thee do we cry, poor banished children of Eve, mourning and weeping in this vale of tears"...

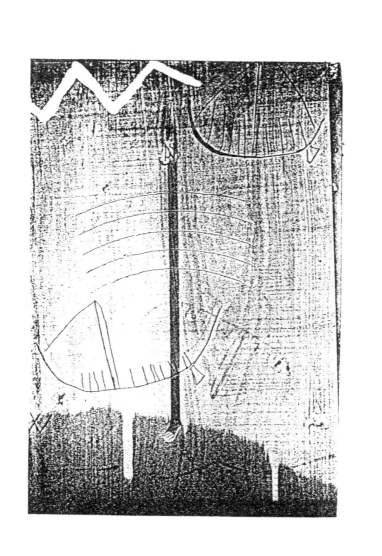

EURE KA!

H O R S E S

They are like strong coursings of wind.

They are like waves of the sea.

They are like the streams that come down
from the mountain — flashing, lingering on
pools, taking thunder out of the rock as they
go.

They eat the grass of our cattle and our
goats and sheep.

Yet one came and took grass from the hand
of a boy. The horse suffered the hand of the
boy through his mane.

Ah, that we were swift and high as birds!
Ah, that we were subtle and shining as the
fish of the lake! That we were winds, waves,
torrents, horses.

That girl has dreamed again. We have a care
and a keeping of the dreams of the girl. The
girl saw in her dream men-horses on the
horizon, going north very fast, the hair blown
back.

Climb the mountain, bring down lengths of snow so I can make gowns and head coverings.

The goatherds and the falconers and the woodmen come down empty handed.

She stamped her foot. She beat them with her small fists. She locked them up. She let them go in the morning.

She sat at the fire. A musician played. *Play the white music.* He played the white music.

A scullion, a girl, cried from the kitchen door,

"The air is all white flowers!"

White blossoms wherever she looked.

Set out vases, bring bowls and cups. Take the sky flowers inside, to my room.

Twenty women ran with tubs and basins, here and there, and carefully brought the heaps of white roses in to the fires.

Make me a coat of white flowers.

One snowflake drifted on to her wrist and

died there and was a glittering ghost.

She stood for an hour under the falling snow. Some say she stood there all day, all winter, all her life long, and when spring came she was not there, she was dissolved in light.

But we know the truth: the princess became a cruel queen. A thousand horsemen died in her wars. Her bitter fires consumed this lover and that.

Once a silver prince came to visit me, said the old queen. *I sent him away.*

It never snowed in that land again.

The mountain summits, they were white always.

C O A L

"Go, cut wood," said the abbot of New Botyl. "The old monks are cold in the crypt."

Brother Jerome was afraid. Thrice he had seen black stones in the snow. He had kicked them aside. There was always another devil-stone beside the river.

Ah, it was the same stone, but it had changed shape! The black stone would beset him always, wherever he went. His foot would stumble on the black stone. The last time, his neck would break, the devil would have him.

Cut wood, in the snow, in the heart of winter, for the old monks with the blue shivering hands!

Out went Brother Jerome, with the axe, towards the bridge and the trees on the other side of the Esk river.

The black stone! Bigger than ever, flashing blue-black out of the snow.

Jerome took the stone and clutched it to him and went staggering back, and down the steps into the crypt where the old monks were, and threw the black stone among the feeble flames.

"Fool!" cried the old monks. "You have killed the fire!"

The stone lay in a nest of flames.

The stone cracked open. A net of dancing light went over the gray crypt walls.

The faces of the old monks flushed.

W H E E L

Rollers cracked and broke, they shattered
under the weight of Brodgar stones.

A boy considered one winter the circuit of
stars and the winter sun-wheel.

The twelfth stone sank in the bog. There they
had lost it, the logs being rags and
shreds, after summer rains.

The mind of the boy cut a log into slices. He
marked the sign of the cut log on the
sand of a loch verge. The quarrymen
laughed. The boy considered the circle
of the year. The boy said, "The life of
a man is but one turn of a wheel."

They considered that the stone circle on the
moor could not be completed, too
much strength was drained. "Young
men broken cannot fish or plough."

The boy considered the sheer rim of the
drinking cup, how — held against the
sun's rim — it brimmed with rainbows
and the promise of rainbows.

"And now we have a keener edge cutting the great star stones in Vestrafiold."

And three generations after that, a poet of the wheel sang the song of the stone-cutters.

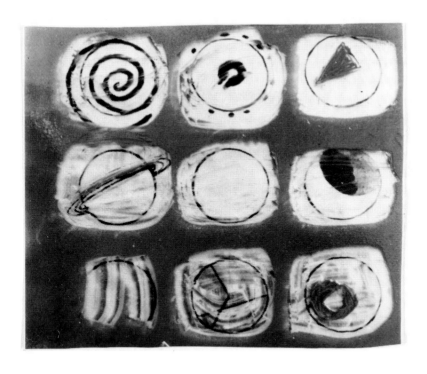

T O B A C C O

Twenty nights hidden they watched the old
one.

He set the leaves on the hot stones. He stirred
them with a stick.   They crackled, crackled.

The old one looked around. A little fire
burned. He threw the dry leaves on to the
embers. Smoke rose up. He bent over the
smoke with eyes closed. The smoke washed
his face. He drew it swirling in at his nose and
mouth. One night the old one nearly died of
coughing. Next night he was at it again,
fearfully and wonderingly.

   The old one would not say where he had
found the leaves. They keep him locked in his
hut.

Three boys bent over the embers and the
shrivelling smoking leaves. Their eyes wa-
tered, they laughed, they sat tranquil, with

folded hands.

Then the old man told them where the plant grew.

Then the cutter of stone hollowed a stone to be a nest for the smouldering leaf. He bored a hole in the side of the tobacco stone. Then each man drew smoke from the stone, one after the other. They kissed the stone, over and over.

This was considered more seemly than the gasping, choking, and eye-waterings over the fire.

They honoured the old tobacco-man with a song, later.

It was *"woman"* and *"woman"* and *"woman"* and *"woman"* and *"woman"*. I was a child.

There was then *"the woman with the big teeth"* and *"the woman with the cheese-press"* and *"the woman who smells of fish."*

There is she who sits at the fire like a sack of old sticks.

They say, "Your mother, the good woman, is dust in a jar."

Why do the women shriek and yell for ordinary mishaps, a rotten gull's egg or the fire hissing and losing its red tongue under a pot or a man sleeping long? But when the well is dry and a boat has not returned, they stand like stones, near and far.

Girls are noisier than birds. Girls shine like mackerel. I do not wish to be closer to the girls.

The sack of sticks, she is your grandmother. The sweetest berries, fresh ewe milk, are put in at the dry twigs of the mouth of the grandmother.

There is a woman who keeps a hundred
names of the people that used to be here.
Their spirits enter her. They shake speech
from her mouth. They move in her head and
hands. *The woman who tells the stories.*

There is a woman who whispers things from
door to door.

I saw yesterday the fisherman's girl that
walks on the shore. The sea draws back. She
follows the sigh of the sea. These are the
games that the girl and the sea play. The sea
gathers itself and laughs and sings up the
stones and washes over the feet of the girl.

The uselessness of girls is become a wonderment since flood tide this morning.

One day, at sunset, a young woman will go
from a door to the door of a young man with
a honeycomb on a dish.

Why have they told me this? Old sack of
sticks, why have I thought all day of a girl
dancing in a wave?

Can honey be gathered from wastes of sea?

V I N L A N D

Leif said, "There is land in the west."

Then they mocked Leif.

The sailors looked deep into Leif's eyes, curling their lips. "It is a speck of soot in your eye, Leif."

Leif said, "If you were to put out my eyes, and char my tongue with hot iron, and break my ankles so that I could not walk nor dance in the new place, yet my nose quivers like a butterfly with smell of crushed grasses in the west."

Next morning Rolf said, "I hear the noise of a breaking wave in the west, under the horizon. Now the sound of many waves. They fall. I listen. Listen."

Then they were eager to mock the ear of Rolf.

Before sunset the helmsman plucked a branch out of the sea.

At midnight they had trouble pushing at a
reef with oars and hands. The right hand of
Rolf bled.

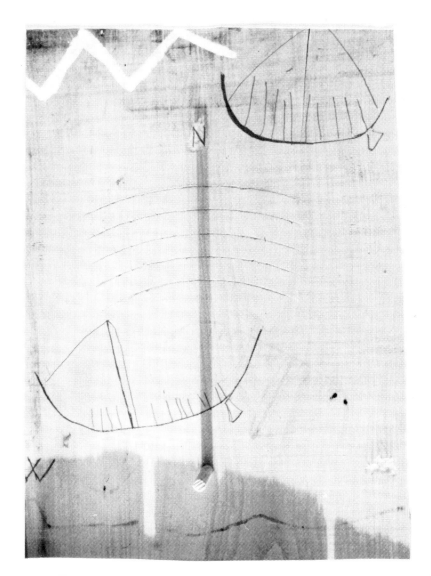

A   N E W   P L A Y

The king weeps. He weeps over his book of
    Latin verbs and his schoolroom text of
    Sophocles. A page glitters, is a gray
    damp stain soon.

The poet walks through an April field. His
    hand is a cluster of grass and daffodils,
    wet with dew. The poet, a boy still,
    closes his fingers on a thorn.

The king looks from the battlement on to a
    shore of witches and Danish cargoes.
    "Your majestie, envoys from the lord
    chancellor of England"...

The poet walks from tavern to tavern. "The
    queen is dead, long live the king"...
    How shall a prince celebrate a broken-
    tongued poet out of the barbarous
    north?

The king turns the book of the sorrows of the
monarchs. The little queen dead bet-
wixt Norway and Scotland. The king
hacked by English steel at Flodden.
Alexander and his horse, broken under
a cliff. The queen his mother beside
axe and block in an English keep.
Duncan.

"Master Will Shakespeare, poet and gentle-
man, begs leave to present to the king's
high majestie the new tragedy of Mac-
beth, wherein are shewn tyrant's ruin
and the fair shoot of kingship that
grew therefrom..."

G U N P O W D E R

First they fought as the beasts fought. Men learned to fight with ceremony. The vanquished bowed their heads. They bled and lay cold in death. The confusion was called now: *battle.*

Stones and pointed sticks were brought to the place of combat. The fountains of the blood were broken. The poet sang: *those were beautiful and heroic ceremonies.*

They have made arrows to soar like birds. Chariot wheels go over bones, over jars and children. In one city is women's weeping. In the neighbouring city are flags and music. Names are carved in stone: the heroes. Horns of ceremony are blown.

Word has come, the walls of the town under the mountain were broken not with horses and battering rams and catapults, but with exploding powder.

Will the poets celebrate a shameful thing?

The cunning of men has overset the wine-jar of ceremony.

T O B A C C O (ii)

So they held Sammy and Rab put a woodbine in his mouth.

Sammy spat it out.

Five times Sammy spat the woodbine out.

The sixth time Sammy was too exhausted and they held a lighted match to the tip and in a back-draught of rage a quantity of smoke got into Sammy's bronchials and lungs.

How Rab and Tommy laughed!

Sammy coughed and sweated all the way home.

He sat down and coughed a piece of his innocence out.

"I'd like you guys to meet the mainstay of the film we're going to make here on this lovely island — Samuel Innertoon."

The director and the camera crew and the lighting men could hardly see the old gray man for the hanks of pipe smoke. It was like a sea-haar drifting about their heads.

The girl secretary put a bottle of gray malt whisky on the table.

"Mr Innertoon here — Sam — knows more about the ballads and lore of this place than any man alive. What we're going to do is this..."

Those whose eyes were not stung to brimming blindness could see what seemed a flawed ruby in the heart of the fog. The jewel fluttered and was the ghost of a flame. More wreaths and wraiths of smoke covered the head of the story-teller.

The assistant lighting man sought, gasping, the glittering frost out of doors.

Squelchings and burblings came from Samuel Innertoon's clogged ghost of a pipe.

Said Mrs Maggie-Bella Innertoon; "Sam always has a smoke before his breakfast. Then it's smoke smoke smoke with him till bed time. The rafters in here are well seasoned. Sam's been smoking since a boy. If he sees Michaelmas he'll be 97."

One by one the television crew sought the diamond of the sun.

I   *R*   *O*   *N*

A small rock, heavy, with a red smear through it. The hunter held it out to them. They laughed.

They went away, faces screwed with laughter.

He did not return to the village. Many were glad.

"It was the eagle took my lamb. I climbed half-way round the mountain, going up. Could I grasp the eagle like a flower?

Half-way down, I heard music of the sun in a cave. I was more frightened of the music than of the eagle. The sun sang. The cave was full of the black songs of the sun.

Inside the cave was a pulsing heart and three shadows. Smoulderings, strikings, mid-earth music, sun-songs. A trough hissed like a nest of snakes. The hunter, he who left us last year, he lifted from the fire and water a long heavy pointed clanging shaft. A boy set the spear against the wall beside a broth-pot and a helmet. They glinted here and there like the scales of fish. The spear shivered with light among the shadows of the cave."

C A N N E D   M E A T

And the voice above the sea surge
*No letting of nets into the sea. The sailors
that sail into the future shall have new food.*

And they broke through the circle of ice. And
the voice again, with the creakings of
rope and sail
*White birds are all about us. Look there, a
whale. But that was food for all the old
sailors that suffered and drowned, not for
us discoverers.*

And they anchored off a cape, with
— one star lit and wolves howling.
— And the voice in that death time.
*Old ways cling yet about us. It may be we
must suffer in an old fashion before we break
through into golden times and our bodies
can endure the new manna and nectar. As,
today we bury in iron-dark earth two young
sailors.*

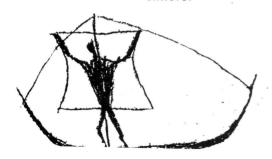

The north was strewn with empty cans: they
flamed across the ice, small slow scat-
tered fires.

So they rowed the wise man to the island of secrets: earth, air, water, fire. There was no rain that summer. Wisdom might unlock the door of water.

They bade the wise man be quick with his water key. They could hear shoals of cod under the horizon, hesitating. The shoals might turn north.

The wise man walked one way with his branch across the island and again another way. A leaf came out and shivered on the branch.

Water was silent. Air spoke to him.

Now the fishermen could hear the chuckling and jostling of the fish, this side of the horizon. The wind blew from north-west. They could hear the under-water cod songs.

"They veer north. The fish are leaving us."

The wise man stood on the shore of the island.

The only change was that the coat of the wise man had been changed to a wide gray square.

The wise man bade the tallest strongest oarsman stand in the prow and hold the top corners of the sheet with his arms spread wide and he bade the two boys that bailed sea water to kneel and hold fast the bottom corners.

The wind struggled to get into the coat. The wind dallied and made itself flat in the stretched coat. The wind sang and flapped and made urgent thrustings in the coat.

A fleck of spindrift stung the helmsman on the mouth.

"We have not known the boat to go faster."

Soon they took in a hundred great fish on the hooks.

Still it did not rain. They dug a new well, deep.

"Make coats for the sea wind to live in, fishermen. Get a long tree to hang the coats on."

So they rowed into Scotland and rowed back with twelve masts.

There was a house in Skara Brae where the hollow stones were kept. The hollow stones were brought to the table four times in the year. The stones were sacred. They were brought to the table at the four sun stations. Boys with clean hands carried the ceremonial stones between the house of the stones and the sun table.

Hollow stones! Nothing is so beautiful as the hollow of the hand. Knuckles and fingers shine, the good drops linger and fall. The mouth drinks. The hand glitters with salt. The hand flows into a hundred shapes. It streams in winter with stars and shadows and the hair of the girls.

Yet soon the hand was a star of bones: after two or three winters soaked in pain.

What was the boy doing with fire and clay? Who was the boy? They had not let that boy carry the hollow stones. The boy sat alone.

One hollow stone held salt, and one water,
and one honey, and one oil and fish, and one
ox blood, on the sun table.

In the time of the equal lights, when the
grass thins, and the sun has silver threads in
his beard, a boy sits between fire and wet clay.
Comely are his hands. They dance about the
lump of clay.

"The duck. Something has gone wrong with the duck. The duck has gone mad."

One duck in the flock.

A mush of old rotting wheat. (A good harvest. Too few mouths.)

"Burn that extra wheat before it stinks."

There, because of the burner's laziness, the wheat lay and rotted at the gate of winter.

The rain fell in torrents. The rain fell on the ruined pile of wheat and made a little pool.

One duck out of the score, it turned aside and it nuzzled and guzzled and began to quack strange quacks. It staggered. It tried (I swear) to dance. It fell.

"No. If we eat that duck, the madness will pass into us too."

The village Good-for-Nothing, he has been eyeing that mush and rottenness all morning. Dare he dip a finger, curl a tongue?

At the end of six winters, all the village could dance and pipe and fight and fall. The gray liquor lay in six stone jars.

Such gray faces, on the morning of the plough!

U R A N U S

On Uranus, a deputation was waiting for them.

The first man had stepped out of the ship, and was about to say immortal words to the millions listening back on Earth, when he became aware that a large crowd was waiting all round the ship.

And they looked just like the folk back home.

A Uranian stepped forward with a piece of paper in his hand. "Earth men", he said. "I welcome you on behalf of the people of Uranus."

In the space centre on earth, they waited for the historic words. Nothing. Silence. The cosmonaut on the screen, half down the ladder, was looking here and there: the address locked in his throat, it seemed.

"We've lost sound," said the sound controller in the space centre. "Temporarily."

On the screen, the surface of Uranus was like a wilderness of banana skins, cold porridge, old boots, empty tins, and mounds of plastic.

"I am commanded to bring you," said the Uranian spokesman, "into the presence of the President of Uranus."

A band played, trumpets drums fifes.

At the first notes of the music of the sphere, the skipper of the space ship shrivelled like a moth in a furnace. And the space ship melted and was a stain on the surface of Uranus.

The band played on. A conductor conducted. The crowd cheered.

In the space centre, the hundred screens went blank. One man, a Doctor Copernicus, suffered a heart attack, and died before sunset, despite a hundred wild kisses of life.

"Attempts are being made to re-establish contact with Uranus."

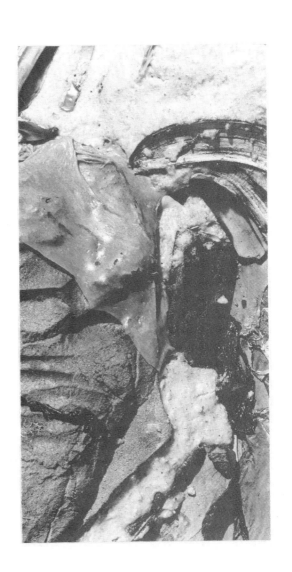

F L I G H T

I whirled down. I brushed dew from morning flowers. A nettle bit me.

Wind cried *"yes"* to the wings, and *"yes"*, urging me up, over the roof, over the orchard.

I am lost in a cloud.

I stand on the cloud, dancing, my eyes dazzle, I stand on the first step of the sun.

I stand on the fourth sun step.

I can see below, between two clouds like marble women, the city and the labyrinth.

Wind rushes into the wings.

I am above islands, in slow circles, now the sea is under my head, now sun fastens sandals about my ankles.

I stand on the seventh step.

Ships crawl across the ocean with wings and oars, burdened.

A ploughman looks at the boy flying. The
oxen stop, they are like beetles.

I stand, in a pirouette, above the city Troy,
tower and battlement and circling chariots.

Seven swans flew below. They called, "Go
down, proud boy." I went up and lingered on
the twelfth step of the sun.

Oh father, leave your gold and your talents
and your intricate house to your other children. To this son you have given freedom and
flight.

I am to go soon into the temple of the sun.

The winged horse flew below, bearing poems.
"O boy, there will be songs about this daring
dance. A thousand girls, boy, will love you,
grieving for this day."

I go higher.

What I long for: to walk among the ringing
star-streets, to have words with Castor and the
Bull, to touch the sword of Orion.

The sun stands high above. It is noon. I burn. My shoulders sweat like candles.

No haste nor hindrance, I can dance down, I can go into the sea and rise again refreshed.

I could sink among the snows of the mountains of Asia.

Prometheus, I will kiss your chain, going past.

No: I would knock on the many-chambered gold halls of the sun. Not even the gods have the key to that door.

The sun birds are all about me: "Higher, rise higher."

I kneel on the fifteenth step of the sun. My tongue is a flame.

How many steps to the door of the Temple of the Sun. "A thousand"... "Ten thousand"... "Go higher, soon"... "Be resolute".

What is the plume that flutters and burns far below in the gray gulf?

I am above the wind.

I will rest here.

Presently I will go slowly up to the seven-teenth step.

But first I will go down among the shepher-desses of Thessaly. They have jars of water. They have leaves to put upon scalds.

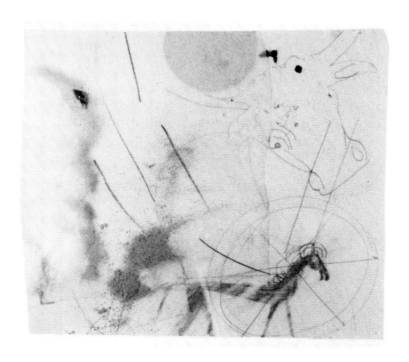

H A R P

Horns groaned here and there. The men blew wind into bladders of pig and cow and let it snarl between their fingers. Children blew thin cries out of grass blades.

A dance. Clapped hands, earth beatings till the feet are sore.

Who has heard the watery songs of trout and crab?

One man heard the thrum of whales. Beyond Suleskerry, he heard whale music.

Death music. With horns and pig bladders and thud of feet and screechings of women they brought the great hunters and the maidens and the wise star-readers to the hewn tombs.

There was a young man and he seized a swan in the still shallows of the loch when the swan was iced in and could not fly and the swan thrashed at him and the swan broke a bone in his side and soon the swan struck out the boy's eyes with a wingclap but still the boy held on to the swan and the swan cried once and was still. When the people came to where that sound was they found the young man with a harp in his hands.

Children plucked new grass blades. They made the slitted grasses shrill like insects.

Shipmen from east brought a drum. The drum, beaten, was like the wakening heart of the world.

The old harper goes from village to village with his music. A boy leads him.

C A T H L E E N

What met the young voyagers at a rock in the
    west?
    A very ancient one, the face hidden,
    who wept, the unending mother tears.

Music in the stretched mouths of the hunters,
    bell music of hounds on the mountain.
    A woman stood beside the stag with
    bitter reproaches.

Ah, they will put the spades in here, for the
    rings and the red gold long kept and
    hidden here for them against the day
    of settlement.
    The turf turned, a cold face was there
    under the russet braids, with dim gold
    at the throat.

Bitter the battle, the host broken, all Ireland
    broken under the Saxon arrows and
    hooves

Ireland takes a fisherman-soldier, she lays the
  green leaves on his wounds, young
  beautiful one, with laughter and con-
  solation, the bride. She lights for him
  lamp and fire.

T O B A C C O *(iii)*

There's room in the hold for one more box
    of ingots, captain. But one. Or the ship
    will sink.

Make room for that barrel with the dark com-
    pression of leaves, the sweetsmelling cask.

These will make the king the roundest yellow-
    est escudos, good chimers.

Set me on board the plantation, wind-dried,
    steeped in Jamaican oil, with molasses.
    Handle it carefully.

Skipper, this cart has come by dangerous
    ways, the bullion was first melted down
    from jars and lamp-brackets, far back,
    in the lost city.

Let but a stave of the cask come loose, let sea salt come near it, it will go hard with you, lieutenant of the embarkation.

T H R O N E

At the meetings, we squatted on stones in a ring. We chewed the knuckle of wisdom. One squatted with purple on his shoulders, the old chief.

This shameful thing happened at the winter council. the young man "hunter of antelopes" sat on a rock. The circle was broken. His legs hung free. He had uprooted himself. He sat on a sun step.

"Hunter of antelopes" was sent into the forest. Has he died in the forest? Has he become an antelope? A girl runs weeping among the huts.

The elder with the purple coat, he was led to the rock. He dominated the circle. Let the young man stand in snow on the summits, this is the sun rock, where the feet are free. Here sun wisdom is given out, in an old thin voice.

Workers in wood, hewers and smokers and carvers, the old man in the purple coat is often weary on his stone, at the council. He puts his hand to the arch of his back. He groans. It is a hard thing to govern hunters and shepherds and the women who urge and prompt darkly.

He sits. He utters the sun wisdom.

F I R E

And they travelled on, they of shining teeth, the hunters, and the toothless old and the children.

And drank blood of wild boar. And so strengthened, went on.

A young woman sang of a burning mountain. There, there, winter will not rot this people. There, for the sun had blessed and crowned the mountain with fire, for those that hunted about the foothills it would be summer always and the warmth and fullness of summer.

In the forest, three hunters did not come back.

Lamentation under the darkening boughs. But the high voice sang and sang, *Burning mountain.*

And *burning mountain* sang when rain fell through the forest on the people, and feet sank into the bog to the knees, and the old were carried across, and five were lost in the wide river beyond the forest.

There was the plain, with herds of wild goats, and the caves in a cliff. There was the horizon, no burning mountain.

Then the horizon blurred with rain. They got shelter in three caves.

The hunters went out in rain against the goats and came back, burdened. They nourished themselves on blood and raw meat. Women took the pelts, they rolled the skins and spoke the ancient words upon them. And they would not let the *"burning mountain"* woman touch a skin. There was yet no sun or wind to dry the the goat skins.

The wise ones considered the mouth that had sung *"burning mountain"*. At night, many words, while the hunters slept, whether a stone be put over that mouth or whether that tongue knew a truth beyond their kenning.

It was now the ninth day of rain. And the thunder began to speak to the people. And they trembled. And flashes came out of the throat of thunder and a tree outside groaned and flamed and smouldered.

A hunter awoke, he stirred, he ran out into the storm. He tore a flaming bough from the struck tree and he brought it into the cave. The people covered their eyes and turned away from the branch that was a burning bird.

The burning bird died. It drowned in the rain.

A messenger from the mountain, cried the witch. The mountain has sent a fire-bird to greet us.

"The rain drowned it," sang the other woman. "Water is our friend."

The old men uttered the wise words. Thunder spoke, his mouth flashed, far away.

The hunter with the smoking stick blew on it and blew on it and sparks flew out and his throat swelled and a flame smoked and un-furled bright on the branch.

Then he gave the messenger from the mountain of summer to the old man who saw to the cutting-up of carcases.

Other titles of the author published by Balnain Books:

THE LOOM OF LIGHT
A CELEBRATION FOR MAGNUS
LETTERS TO GYPSY